Dedicated to the memory of my dad who spent his lifetime "spinning" poetry and enchantment. And to those father/daughter dances, my five year old feet atop of his.

-Raven

SPIN
A
CIRCLE

MacLaren-Cochrane Publishing, Inc.

Text©2021 Raven Howell
Cover and Interior Art©2021 Ann Pilicer

Spin a Circle! Dyslexic Edition

MCPInfo@Maclaren-Cochranepublishing.com

Library of Congress Control Number: 2020949723

First Edition

ISBN
Hardcover: 978-1-64372-054-8
Softcover: 978-1-64372-056-2

For orders, visit

www.MCP-Store.com
www.maclaren-cochranepublishing.com
www.facebook.com/maclaren-cochranepublishing

By Raven Howell

Illustrated by Amy Pilicer

SPIN A CIRCLE

Spin a circle,
Sing a rhyme,
Weeble, wobble,
Baby time!

Spin a circle,
Sing a rhyme,
Paint and play,
It's toddler time!

Spin a circle,
Off to school,

a   *SKIP*   and

JUMP

provide the fuel!

UP AND DOWN

Slowly rising,
Up I go,
Then touching down
On tippy-toe.

Dipping low,
Springing high,
We teeter-tot
From earth to sky!

BALL

I kick it.
I roll it.

It bounces off the
wall.

I toss it in the air,
and reach and catch
my ball.

...And sometimes
my puppy does.

READ!

Read on the farm,
Read in town.
Flip a cartwheel,
Read upside down!

MAKING MUSIC

Clap your hands, twirl and dance,
Giddy-up, giddy-up, leap and prance!

Tap a drum, pluck a string.
Toot a flute and sing, sing, sing!

WHAT SHOULD WE DO TODAY?

Should we trot like horses?

Clomp, clomp, clomp

Should we trudge like elephants?

Stomp, stomp, stomp

Should we chirp like
birds do?
Tweet, tweet, tweet

Should we skip and jump

On our own two feet?

GRANDPA'S DAY

Pick me up to piggyback.
Lift me high upon your back.

Ride me, sway me
In the breeze.
Gallop me
Among the trees.

Grampa, hum my favorite song
While I bounce and bob along.

A BUMPY RIDE

Hoe, sow,
Dig, dig, dig.
We ride in Pa's
wheelbarrow rig.

Bump

bump

bump

Through flowered garden.
Hi ladybugs—
We beg your pardon!

BOX OF BLOCKS

One by one,
I stack them wide,
Pile them higher,
Side by side.

Loading,
heaping
blocks,
and then—
Knock them
down
to...
start again!

FINGER PAINTING

Smear red fingers,
Blot five cars.
Streak blue skies
With shooting stars.

Paint zigzags
Of city road.
Splash to country green
With toad.

A yellow thumb?
Smudge a sun!
Swirl and splotch
In rainbow fun!

MY BOX

I shake it gently — bump, bump, bump,
Tap the top — thump, thump, thump.
Pull it down, lift it up, shake from side to side.
Reach in, tug,
Cuddle, hug.
Look who hides inside!

FOLLOW THE LEADER

I'm the leader,
Follow me.
Bend your elbow.
Tap your knee.

Stand up tall. Hike in place.
Put a smile upon your face.

Now what would you like to do?
You can be the leader, too!

SAND

I curl my fingers, cup my hand.
Spoon in, scoop out silky sand.

Fill my pail up to the top.
Dig, dip, lift, drop.

Shoo, ladybug!
Shoo, little ants!
Shoo, tickly sand–

Out of my pants!

HIPPETY-HOP

In chalky squares
I hippety-hop,
Up and down,
No time to stop;

Hopscotch, 4-square,
I don't care,

I like to jumpety-jump in the air!

SOMERSAULTING

Fluff a pillow on the ground.
Make yourself a little round.
Tilt your head as you begin.
Tip and tumble. Tuck your chin.
Over now- heels in the air.
Somersault if you dare!

SEED
(CAN YOU DO THIS?)

Tiny seed,
In it goes.

Pat the soil,

Let it doze.

Springtime comes, seed wakes up
Yellow as a buttercup!

YOGA MOVES

I stretch around and twist.
I bend to touch my toes.

I lift into a triangle,

A "Downward Doggy" pose.

My breath is slow and
deep,
Focused now, and calm,
I balance on one foot
And reach up with my
palms.

My hands and arms are branches
And when I lift them high,
I'm strong and solid as a tree
Between the earth and sky.

FAMILY TREASURES

Babies laugh,
babies cry,
they smile hello and
wave bye-bye.

They sip, they gurgle, drool and dribble,
crawl and creep, and screech and
scribble.

My sister stands, then
plops back down,
she bursts in giggle,
burps and frowns.

At last she sleeps, head on my shoulder,
and makes me smile as I hold her.

CATCH YOUR BREATH

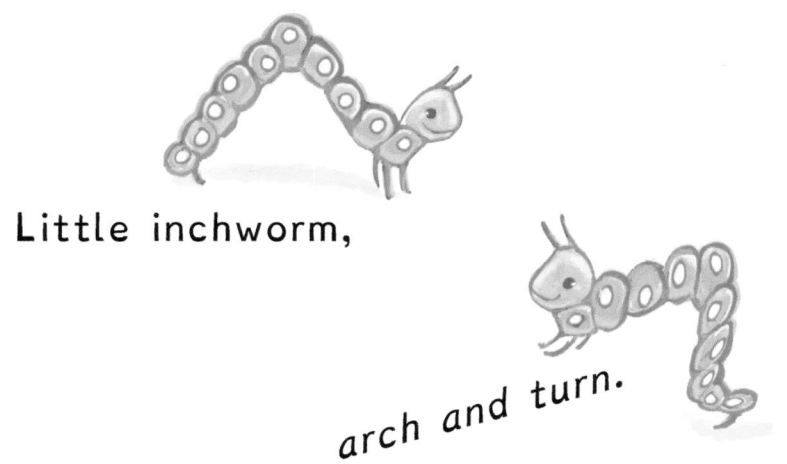

Little inchworm,

arch and turn.

Pinch your green-ness
on the fern.

Inch up on my
outstretched finger,

Then we both can sit and linger.

MAKING A FORT

Blankets draped across a chair,
Walls of quilt engulf my lair.
The ends tuck in the sofa's side
To keep the roof sturdy and wide.

My private cave,
My secret space,
My palace made of cloth and lace.

CHASING LEAVES

"Catch my colors!"

Autumn sings
In auburn leap
And scarlet swing!

SNOW STORM

Snowflakes glaze me
Head to toe.
I shimmy, I sparkle,
I romp through the snow.
My mouth opens wide,
Catching cold flakes
In the glittering flurry
The falling snow makes.

Then *crackle* and *crunch*,
I stomp ice on the gound.
I make a snow angel
And pack a snow mound.

Ready for cocoa,
It's time to get warm.
We'll come out again
The next snow storm.

NIGHTTIME'S SONG

This teddy bear will swing, swing, swing,
Cuddled tight in my arms as I sing, sing, sing,
Draped in a dream moon's melody brings
With star bell chimes,

And lullaby rings.

Raven Howell - Author

Raven has written several award-winning picture books for children. Her poetry is found in kids'
magazines such as Highlights for Children, Humpty Dumpty, The School Magazine, and Ladybug. She is
the Creative & Publishing Advisor for RedClover Reader and writes The Book Bug column for Story
Monsters Ink magazine. Raven is inspired by nature, whimsical art, kindness, and laughter. She's
particular to family time, Scrabble games, morning yoga, and reading a good book in the sunshine.

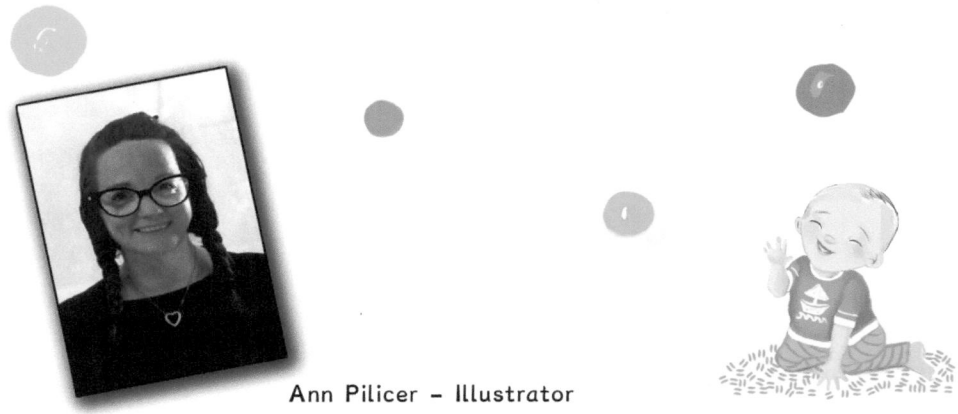

Ann Pilicer - Illustrator

Ann Pilicer received her BFA in Illustration from Parsons School of Design in New York City. She
has illustrated a number of children's books and works both digitally and traditionally in gouache
and watercolor, using playful bold strokes of color. She has the ability to vary her style, giving each
book a look all it's own. Her goal is to create children and creatures, both big and small, that gleam
with character and put smiles on faces of all ages. She hopes that her artwork can inspire young,
budding artists to create. Ann has art direction and book design experience and loves having a hand
in bringing it all together. She lives in Florida with her husband and two beautiful girls.

What is Dyslexie Font?

Each letter is given its own identity making it easier for people with dyslexia
to be more successful at reading.

The Dyslexie font:
1 Makes letters easier to distinguish
2 Offers more ease, regularity and joy in reading
3 Enables you to read with less effort
4 Gives your self-esteem a boost
5 Can be used anywhere, anytime and on (almost) every device
6 Does not require additional software or programs
7 Offers the simplest and most effective reading support

The Dyslexie font is specially designed for people with dyslexia, in order
to make reading easier – and more fun. During the design process, all
basic typography rules and standards were ignored. Readability and
specific characteristics of dyslexia are used as guidelines for the design.

Graphic designer Christian Boer created a dyslexic-friendly font to make reading easier for people
with dyslexia, like himself.

"Traditional fonts are designed solely from an aesthetic point of view," Boer writes on his website,
*"which means they often have characteristics that make characters difficult to recognize for people
with dyslexia. Oftentimes, the letters of a word are confused, turned around or jumbled up because
they look too similar."*

Designed to make reading clearer and more enjoyable for people with dyslexia, Dyslexie uses heavy
base lines, alternating stick and tail lengths, larger openings, and semicursive slants to ensure that
each character has a unique and more easily recognizable form.

Our books are not just for children to enjoy, they are also for adults
who have dyslexia who want the experience of reading
to the children in their lives.

Learn more and get the font for your digital devices at
www.dyslexiefont.com

Get books in Dyslexie Font at: www.mcp-store.com

| 3 | Hold my Hand | Short sentences, familiar words, and simple concepts for children eager to read on their own but still need help. |

CPSIA information can be obtained
at www.ICGtesting.com
Printed in the USA
BVHW020840150321
602548BV00013B/209